Marcy Schaaf

The Great Egg-scape:

A Chicken Island Adventure - Part 2

Welcome back to Chicken Island, where feathers fly and adventures abound! In this egg-citing sequel to "The Chicken Island Adventure," our plucky poultry pals find themselves in a feathery frenzy like never before. When the chickens catch a case of Brodie Fever and decide they'd rather be mamas than egg layers, it's up to Farmer Fred and his clever companions to hatch a plan to get them back on track. Join us as we embark on a journey filled with laughter, friendship, and plenty of egg-squisite surprises. So grab your feathers and get ready to cluck along because the fun is just beginning on Chicken Island!

Once upon a time, on Chicken Island, feathers were about to ruffle in the most egg-squisite way!

The chickens were acting more scrambled than sunny-side up! Instead of laying eggs, they were nesting...

"What's going on?" exclaimed Farmer Fred, his eyebrows raised.

"We've got a case of Brodie Fever!"
announced Henrietta, clutching a sunflower
seed like it was her firstborn..

"Brodie Fever? Is that contagious?" asked Farmer Fred, backing away cautiously.

The rooster with a beak for brains, strutted forward. "Oh, it's spreading faster than gossip at a coop party!"

"But we need eggs for breakfast, lunch, and dinner!" fretted Farmer Fred, his stomach growling in protest..

"Don't crack up just yet, Farmer Fred! We've got this!" chirped Cheddar.

The chickens huddled together in the coop,

"We need a coop-tastrophe to distract them!" suggested Daisy, twirling a dandelion in her beak.

"Like a hen-sized disco ball!" clucked Fluffy, her feathers practically disco dancing with excitement.

"We could give them egg-laying lessons!" proposed Pecky, doing her best impression of a professor with a beak.

"And a fashion show with the fanciest eggshell hats!" added Cluckington, posing dramatically with an imaginary runway.

The chickens nodded in agreement, their beaks bobbing like they were agreeing with the world's funniest joke..

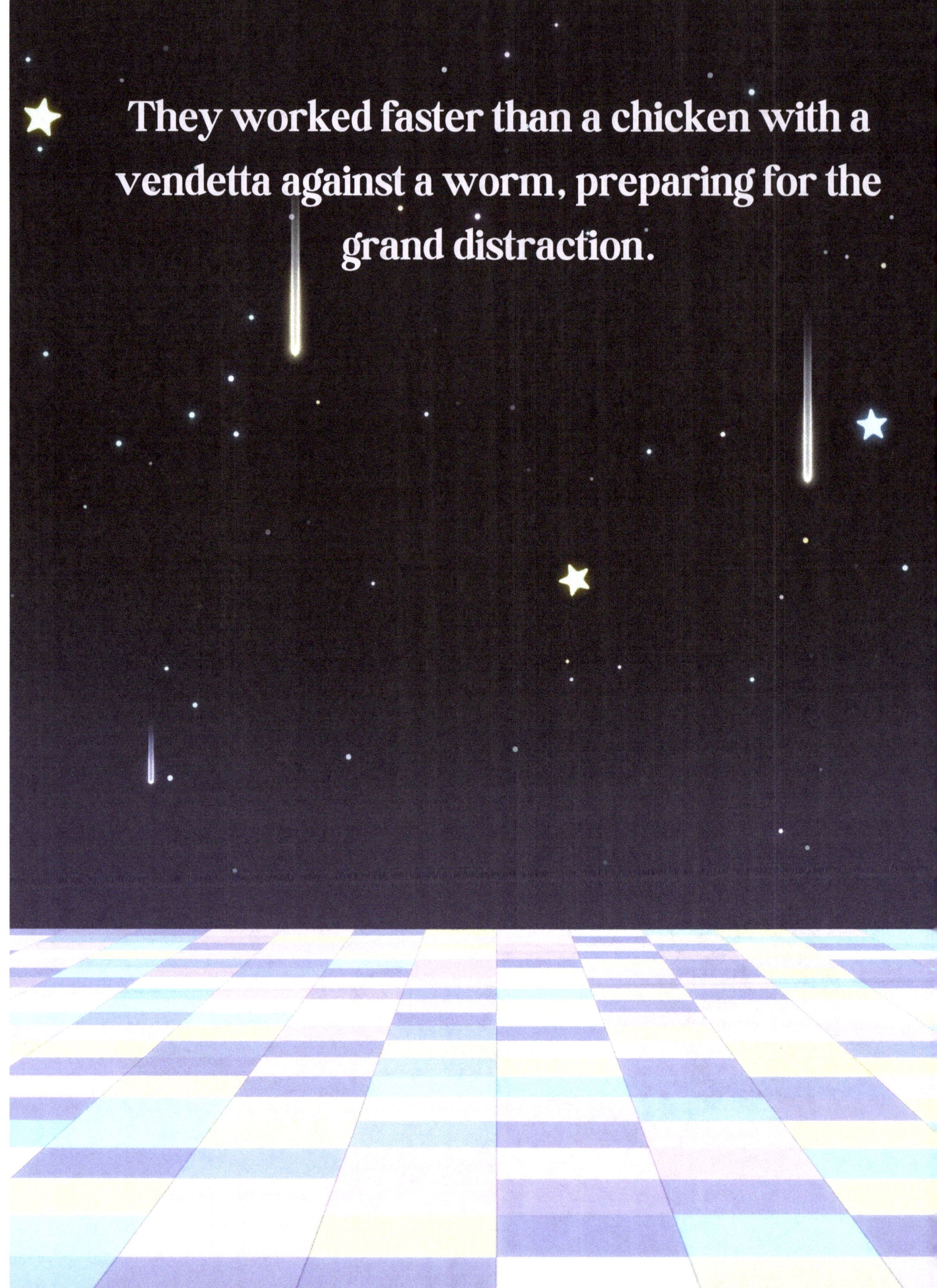
They worked faster than a chicken with a vendetta against a worm, preparing for the grand distraction.

CARNIVAL
When the big day arrived, Chicken Island turned into a coop-tastic carnival of clucks and chuckles.

The chickens rolled eggs like they were competing for the Egg Olympics, aiming for the gold medal in egg rolling.

They danced like nobody was watching, except everybody was watching, so they danced even harder!

Even Farmer Fred got in on the action,
doing the chicken dance with a fervor that
would make any chicken proud !

The distractions worked like magic! The broody chickens forgot all about being mamas and became egg-straordinary egg layers once more.

"Thank you, thank you very much!" Farmer
Fred exclaimed, his heart as warm as a
freshly laid egg.

"Who needs Hollywood when you've got Chicken Island?" chuckled Cheddar, leading a conga line around the coop.

From that day on, Chicken Island was filled with laughter, eggs, and happy clucks, like a permanent party for poultry.

And whenever a chicken felt broody, they knew just what to do—shake their tail feathers and join the fun!

But wait, the end? Not even close! There are more adventures waiting to be hatched on Chicken Island.

So grab your feathers, hold onto your beak, and get ready for another egg-stravaganza!

And remember, there's no problem too scrambled that a little laughter can't unscramble.

The end...

or is it just the beginning of another egg-stravaganza?

Glossary:

Brodie:

A condition where chickens become broody, meaning they want to sit on eggs to hatch them and become mothers.

Egg-squisite:

used to describe something that is exceptionally beautiful, delightful, or finely crafted in relation to eggs. It's a whimsical way to express admiration or appreciation for the quality or appeal of eggs, whether in appearance, taste, or any other aspect.

Egg-straordinary:

It's used to describe something that is exceptionally remarkable, or impressive in a context related to eggs or chickens. In the context of the story, it emphasizes the uniqueness and special qualities of the chickens' egg-related adventures and antics..

Egg-stravaganza:

It refers to a lively and extravagant event or celebration centered around eggs or poultry-related activities. In the context of the story, it emphasizes the exciting and festive nature of the chickens' adventures and the fun-filled activities they partake in, such as egg rolling, dancing, and more..

Egg-citing:

It describes something that is thrilling, enjoyable, or filled with anticipation, particularly in relation to eggs or chicken-related activities. In the context of the story, it emphasizes the excitement and adventure that the chickens experience as they embark on their egg-related escapades.

Egg-ceptional:

It refers to something that is outstanding, extraordinary, or remarkable, particularly in the context of eggs or chicken-related matters. In the story, "egg-ceptional" underscores the remarkable and special qualities of the chickens' adventures and the creative solutions they come up with to overcome challenges.

The actual chickens this story's about!

Books By Schaaf

www.BookBySchaaf.com

Find us at: